TAPESTRY OF LIGHT

A CELTIC CHRISTMAS CELEBRATION

by Joseph M. Martin
Orchestration by Stan Pethel

CONTENTS

Performance Time: Approximately 45 minutes

(1) This symbol indicates a track number on the StudioTrax CD (Accompaniment Only).

Harold Flammer MUSIC

A DIVISION OF SHAWNEE PRESS, INC.
EXCLUSIVELY DISTRIBUTED BY HAL LEONARD CORPORATION

Visit Shawnee Press Online at
www.shawneepress.com

FOREWORD

The music of Christmas is a treasure for both the ear and the heart. Each winter it covers our lives with a hopeful blanket of sound and reminds us that even in the silence of winter, there is song. Each tradition offers its own rich vocabulary of holiday carols joining together faith and art into a glorious fabric of melody and truth. From angelic acclamations to delicate lullabies, the message of God's love leaps from the pages of our songbooks and finds a home in the tender places of our hearts.

Through the singing and sharing of this work, may the grace that inspired these time-honored tunes surround and inspire you. As you light the candles and raise your voices, may the joy and peace of Christ fill you and shine through you. May the Father of all lights gather us all to His heart and weave us into a wonderful tapestry of Light.

JOSEPH M. MARTIN

PROGRAM NOTES

"Tapestry of Light" is a joining of traditional carols, primarily from the British Isles, with scripture reading and candle lighting. I was inspired by recent trips to Ireland, Scotland, Wales and England to create a work that celebrates the rich heritage of seasonal song that is part of this great tradition.

The suggestions indicated in the book are merely templates for you to use as you design your service. Please insert your own holiday traditions when using this work. In providing two different voicing and orchestral options, I hoped to enable choirs of any size to present this work. The inclusion of visual elements and choreography options (Digital Resource Kit) are all optional and are provided as a guide for directors who seek to make their cantata presentations even more creative.

THE LIGHT OF CREATION

more **NARRATOR 1:** *[From off stage in darkness.]*

In the beginning God created the heavens and the earth. The earth was formless and empty. Darkness was over the surface of the deep, and the Spirit of God was hovering over the waters. And God said, "Let there be light," and there was light. *(Gen. 1:1-3 NIV)*

[Raise the lights and light the first candle(s).]

CAROLS OF HOPE AND LIGHT

Words by
JOSEPH M. MARTIN (BMI)

Based on tunes:
I SAW THREE SHIPS
SUSSEX CAROL
IN DULCI JUBILO
Arranged by
JOSEPH M. MARTIN (BMI)

6

TAPESTRY OF LIGHT - SAT

8

Tune: SUSSEX CAROL, Traditional English Carol

TAPESTRY OF LIGHT - SA[

10

TAPESTRY OF LIGHT - SAT

voice._____ Give ye heed to what we say:

"News! News! Soon the Lord___ will come to stay.

To a low - ly cat - tle stall, God will give___ a

Sing to God a ju - bi - lant song! Re-
joice, re - joice, your Light will come on Christ - mas day, on Christ - mas day. Re-
joice, re - joice, your light will come on Christ - mas day in the

THE LIGHT OF PREPARATION

NARRATOR 1:

The voice of one crying in the wilderness: "Prepare the way of the LORD. Make straight in the desert a highway for our God. Every valley shall be exalted; and every mountain and hill brought low. The crooked places shall be made straight; and the rough places smooth. The glory of the LORD shall be revealed; and all flesh shall see it together; for the mouth of the LORD has spoken." *(Isaiah 40:3-5)*

NARRATOR 2:

I, the LORD, have called you in righteousness. I will take hold of your hand. I will keep you and will make you to be a covenant for the people and a light for the Gentiles. *(Isaiah 42:6)*

LONGING FOR THE LIGHT

Words by
JOSEPH M. MARTIN (BMI)

Based on tunes:
SCARBOROUGH FAIR
GREENSLEEVES
Arranged by
JOSEPH M. MARTIN (BMI)

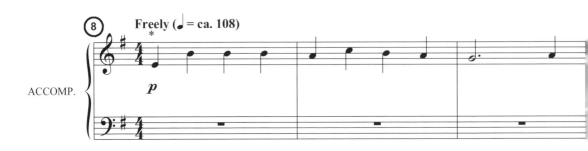

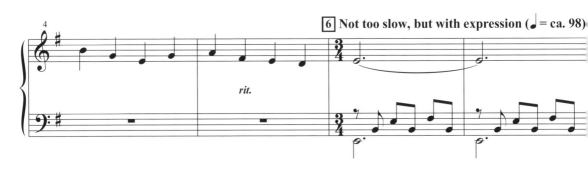

* Tune: VENI EMMANUEL, Plainsong
** Tune: SCARBOROUGH FAIR, Traditional English Melody

Come and ran - som Is - ra - el. _____ Come with pow'r and maj - es - ty. _____ Loose our bonds and set ___ us free. _____

Tune: GREENSLEEVES, Traditional English Melody

TAPESTRY OF LIGH

20

Babe,___ the Son___ of Ma - ry.

Come, O come, great

Lord___ of grace.___ Come, in - hab - it all of our

joice!____ Em - man - u - el____ shall come to thee,____ O Is - ra - el. Re - joice, re - joice!____ The Light will come,____ the Babe,____ the

dim. poco a poco

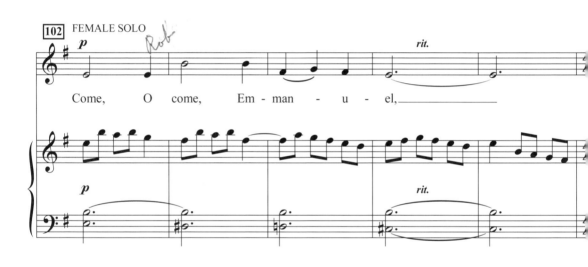

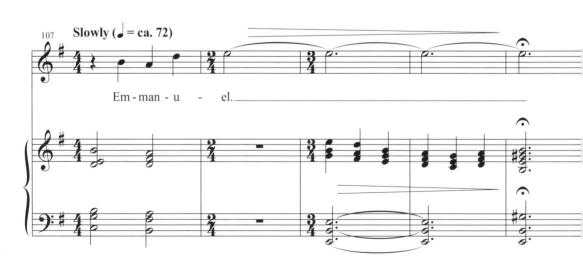

THE LIGHT OF ANTICIPATION

NARRATOR 1:

Hear this promise from scripture:

The desert and the parched land will be glad.
  The wilderness will rejoice and blossom.
Like the crocus, it will burst into bloom.
  It will rejoice greatly and shout for joy.
All will see the glory of the LORD,
  and the splendor of our God. *(Isaiah 35:1-2)*

[Light the next candle(s).]

AN ADVENT GARDEN

Words by
JOSEPH M. MARTIN (BMI)

Tune: **BROTHER JAMES' AI**
by J. L. MACBETH BAIN (1860-192
Arranged b
JOSEPH M. MARTIN (BM

Silent night, HOLY NIGHT!

For unto you is born this day
in the city of David a Saviour,
which is Christ the Lord.

Luke 2:11

CHRISTMAS EVE CANDLELIGHT SERVICE

DECEMBER 24, 2011

Prelude

Welcome

Lighting of the Christ Light

Leader: In the beginning of creation,
When God made heaven and earth,
The earth was without form and void.
Darkness was over the face of the deep,
And a mighty wind swept over the waters.
God said, "Let there be light,"
And there was light.

All: God saw that the Light was good,
And God separated the light from darkness.

Leader: When all things began, the Word already was.
The Word dwelt with God,
And what God was, the Word was.
Through him all things came to be;
No single thing was created without him.
All that came to be was alive with his life,
And that life was the light of the world.

All: The light shines in the darkness,
And the darkness has never put it out.

Prayer: Gracious and loving God, tonight we rejoice that the Light of the World has come into our lives. Illumine us with your Spirit's presence that we would hear and receive the light of Christ as his birth is read and proclaimed. Open our hearts to the wonders of this holy Light. Touch us with its brilliance. We pray in the name of Jesus. Amen

**Hymn No. 1008 "Angels from the Realms of Glory"

The Light of Incarnation: Isaiah 9:6, Luke 2:1-7

O Wondrous Night   choir

Hymn No. 1004 "While Shepherds Watched Their Flocks"

The Light of Declaration: Luke 2:8-14

A Celtic Noel   choir

Reading: *When the World was Dark*

The Light of Revelation: Isaiah 60:1-3, Matthew 2:1-2

Carols of the Quest   choir

**Hymn No. 999 "The First Noel"

The Light of Proclamation: Matthew 5:14-16

A Celtic Gloria   choir   *Remain Standing ?*

Christmas Response
> Leader: *A boy has been born for us;*
> All: A child has been given to us.
> Leader: *And his name shall be called*
> > *Wonderful Counselor, Mighty God,*
> > *Eternal Father, the Prince of Peace.*
> > *Once we were no people;*
> All: Now we are God's people.
> Leader: *Once we walked in darkness;*
> All: New we have seen a great light.

**Candlelighting and "Silent Night"
> Please light your candle from the person next to you and join in as we sing "Silent Night".

As you go forth, may the Light of the World, brighten your darkness. May Christ so shine in us that all will know the Light of everlasting Love.

Resource for Lighting the Christ Light, *When the World was Dark,* and Christmas Response: *Cloth for the Cradle* by Iona Community/Wild Goose Worship Group, copyright 2000.

(W)
Warner
Press

U3482
CHRISTIAN ART®
©Warner Press, Inc
All rights reserved
Made in USA

Song lyrics by Joseph Mohr. Translated by John F. Young.
Photo © Design Pics.com

The gift of love_ sent from a-bove_ will graceful winds will blow.

like a gar-den grow.

The des-ert sands_ will_ come a-live_ as streams be-gin to

flow. The bar-ren lands will bloom and thrive. The hills will be made

low. In ev-'ry place, God's gift of grace will like a gar-den

grow. Al - le - lu - ia! Al - le - lu - ia! Let the

earth lift its voice; for a new rose is__ bloom-ing ⁓ in__

Zi - on. Let the__ gar-den re - joice.

The

grow.

Then

peace,___ like a gar - den, will grow.___

THE LIGHT OF THE ANUNCIATION

NARRATOR 2:

Hear the words of the Prophet:

Therefore, the Lord Himself will give you a sign: the virgin will be with Child and will give birth to a Son, and will call Him Immanuel. *(Isaiah 7:14)*

Now hear words form the gospel of Luke:

God sent the angel Gabriel to Nazareth, a town in Galilee, to a virgin pledged to be married to a man named Joseph, a descendant of David. The virgin's name was Mary. The angel went to her and said, "Greetings, you who are highly favored, the Lord is with you."

Mary was greatly troubled at his words and wondered what kind of greeting this might be. But the angel said to her, "Do not be afraid, Mary. You have found favor with God. You will conceive and give birth to a Son, and you are to call Him Jesus. He will be great, and He will be called the Son of the Most High. The Lord God will give Him the throne of His father David, and He will reign over Jacob's descendants forever. His kingdom will never end." *(Luke 1:26-33)*

THE HOLY CHILD OF MARY

Words by
JOSEPH M. MARTIN (BMI)

Based on tunes:
THE HOLLY AND THE IVY
SANS DAY CAROL
Arranged by
JOSEPH M. MARTIN (BMI))

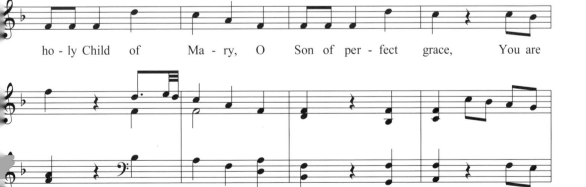

Tune: THE HOLLY AND THE IVY, Traditional English melody

34

peace and love sent from a-bove. You are wor-thy of our praise.

TENOR

BASS

mp unis. **19**

The stars that shine in

heav-en, the snow up-on the trees are pure and bright and

filled with light, but none com-pares with Thee.

legato

won - der of __ heav - en has come to our night. __

The __ Son born of __ Ma - ry __ is

God's per - fect light. No - el, no - el. The __

Son born of __ Ma - ry is __ God's per - fect light.

O ho - ly night of

won - ders, O night when Christ came down, let the earth re-joice with

tune-ful noise and a ju - bi - la - tion sound. Al - le - lu - ia!__ Al - le-

Al - le - lu - ia!

lu - ia!__ Al - le - lu - ia! Al - le - lu - ia! Re - joice!__ Al - le -

Al - le - lu - ia! Al - le - lu - ia! Al - le -

Remain Standing

THE LIGHT OF INCARNATION

NARRATOR 2:

Allen

For unto us a Child is born. Unto us a Son is given; and the government shall be upon His shoulder; and His name shall be called Wonderful, Counselor, the Mighty God, the Everlasting Father, the Prince of Peace. *(Isaiah 9:6)*

NARRATOR 1:

Harriet

In those days Caesar Augustus issued a decree that a census should be taken of the entire Roman world. So Joseph also went up from the town of Nazareth in Galilee to Judea, to Bethlehem, the town of David, because he belonged to the house and line of David. He went there to register with Mary, who was pledged to be married to him and was expecting a child. While they were there, the time came for the Baby to be born, and she gave birth to her firstborn - a Son. She wrapped Him in cloths and placed Him in a manger, because there was no guest room available for them. *(Luke 2:1-7)*

[Light the next candle(s).]

O WONDROUS NIGHT

Words by
JOSEPH M. MARTIN (BMI)

Tune: **LONDONDERRY AIR**
Traditional Irish Tune
Arranged by
JOSEPH M. MARTIN (BMI)

O won-drous night, the stars on high are sing - ing. This is the

night of our dear Sav - ior's birth. O glo - rious

This is the night of our Sav - ior's birth.

voice and tune your heart for praise. O won-drous

night _____ that brought the gift of Je - sus.

O won-drous night that saw the light ___ of ___ grace. _____

44

TENOR or SOPRANO SOLO

O won-drous night, the heav-ens shine with

Oo

glo - ry, beam - ing with light, love paints the shad - ows

gold; and from the heights, the an - gels share the

The shad - ows gold._____ Oo_____

wor - ship! Lift up your voice and tune your heart for praise. O won-drous night_____ that brought the gift of

THE LIGHT OF DECLARATION

NARRATOR 2:

There were shepherds living out in the fields nearby, keeping watch over their flocks at night. An angel of the Lord appeared to them and the glory of the Lord shone around them. They were terrified!

But the angels said to them, "Do not be afraid, for I bring you good news of great joy that will be for all the people. Today, in the town of David, a Savior has been born to you. He is Christ the Lord. This will be a sign to you: you will find a Baby wrapped in cloths, lying in a manger."

And suddenly, a great company of the heavenly hosts appeared with the angel, praising God and saying, "Glory to God in the highest and on earth peace to all people on whom His favor rests." *(Luke 2:8-14)*

[Light the next candle(s).]

A CELTIC NOEL

Words by
MICHAEL BARRETT *and*
JOSEPH M. MARTIN (BMI)

based on tune
CANDLE
FOREST GREE
Arranged
MICHAEL BARRETT (BM
and JOSEPH M. MARTIN (BM

* Tune: FOREST GREEN, Traditional English Melody
** Tune: CANDLER, Traditional Scottish Melody

al - le - lu - ia! Glo - ri - a, glo - ri - a!

Glo - ry to God! No - el, no - el!___ The

song is be - gin - ning with praise and thanks - giv - ing. Sing

"Je - sus is born."

No -

No - el, sing we no -

el, no - el!_____ The an - gels are prais - ing. The

el!_____ Sing we no -

shep - herds are rais - ing their voice to the sky. No -

Glo - ry to God. No - el, no - el!___ God's

light is up - on us. His Word is a - mong us, for

Je - sus is born.

56

sound through cre - a - tion to wel-come the King. Sing___

sound through cre - a - tion to wel-come the King.

al - le - lu - ia, al - le - lu - ia! Glo - ri - a, glo - ri - a!

unis.

Glo - ry to God! No - el, no - el!___ The

unis.

THE LIGHT OF REVELATION

NARRATOR I:

Arise, shine, for your light has come,
  and the glory of the LORD rises upon you.
 See, darkness covers the earth
  and thick darkness is over the peoples,
but the LORD rises upon you
  and His glory appears over you.
 Nations will come to your light,
  and the kings to the brightness of your dawn.
(Isaiah 60:1-3)

NARRATOR 2:

After Jesus was born in Bethlehem in Judea, during the time of King Herod, Magi from the east came to Jerusalem and asked, "Where is the one who has been born king of the Jews? We saw His star when it rose and we have come to worship Him." *(Matthew 2:1-2)*

[Light the next candle(s).]

CAROLS OF THE QUEST

Words by
JOSEPH M. MARTIN (BMI)

Based on tunes:
GARTAN
IRBY
KINGSFOLD
DIX
FOREST GREEN
Arranged by
JOSEPH M. MARTIN (BMI)

* Tune: GARTAN, Traditional Irish Melody
  Words: Christina G. Rossetti, 1830-1894
** Introduction is optional.

Tune: IRBY, Henry John Gauntlett, 1805-1876
Words: Cecil Frances Alexander, 1818-1895

TAPESTRY OF LIGHT -

With the poor, and meek, and lowly,
was a stall.
lived on earth, our Savior holy.

* O

* Tune: KINGSFOLD, Traditional English Melody
  Words: Louis F. Benson, 1855-1930, alt.

TAPESTRY OF LIGHT - SATB

sing a song of Beth - le - hem, of __ seek - ers from __ a -
far who __ trav - eled through the wil - der - ness, in -
spired by heav - en's star. The __ light that shone __ on __

marziale - light and detached

Tune: FOREST GREEN, Traditional English Melody

TAPESTRY OF LIGHT

star of won - der, star___ of___ might, shine down on___ us we

pray.

As with___ glad - ness, kings of old did the guid - ing

star be - hold.

Burn bright your hope - ful mes - sage___ clear in

As with joy they hailed its light,

ev - 'ry heart to - day.

32 lead - ing on - ward, beam - ing bright. O

Morn - ing Star, rise in our lives and lead us to Love's

70

THE LIGHT OF PROCLAMATION

NARRATOR 1:

You are the light of the world. A town built on a hill cannot be hidden. Neither do people light a lamp and put it under a bowl. Instead they put it on its stand, and it gives light to everyone in the house. In the same way, let your light shine before others, that they may see your good deeds and glorify your Father in heaven. *(Matthew 5:14-16)*

[Light the next candle(s).]

A CELTIC GLORIA!

Words by
JOSEPH M. MARTIN (BMI)

based on tune
ASH GROV
ST. DENI
Arranged
JOSEPH M. MARTIN (BM

* Tune: ASH GROVE, Welsh melody

la - tion sing, "Je - sus is born!"

The__ stars__ all are__ sing - ing.__ The
(mel.)

bells__ all__ are__ ring - ing. The__ peo - ple__ are__ bring - ing__ their__

The an - gels on high raise a ju - bi - lant

"Glo - ri - a! Je - sus is born!"

song!

They

"Glo -

soar through the heav - ens with shouts clear and strong!

taking our darkness away. The day shines with

glory as dawn tells the story, for this is the

with grace.

morning God wakes us with, wakes us with grace. Sing,

Lyrics: "Glo - ri - a! Glo - ri - a! Glo - ri - a! Je - sus is born!" Give

praise all cre - a - tion. Re - joice ev - 'ry___ na - tion. With

glad ju - bi - la - tion sing, "Je - sus is

born!"___

THE LIGHT OF CONSECRATION

NARRATOR 1:

Then Jesus spoke to the people, He said, "I am the light of the world, whoever follows me will never walk in darkness, but will have the light of life." *(John 8:12)*

[Light the next candle(s).]

BETHLEHEM LIGHT

Words by
PHILLIPS BROOKS (1835-1893)

Based on tune:
FARE THEE WELL
Traditional Irish Melody
Arranged by
JOSEPH M. MARTIN (BMI)

bove thy deep_ and_ dream - less sleep, the_ si - lent_ stars go

by. Yet_ in thy dark street_ shin - eth the_

ev - er - last - ing_ Light; and all the hopes and fears_ of_

all the years are_ met_ in_ thee to - night.

en - ter in. Be___ born___ in___ us to - day. We___

hear the Christ - mas___ an - gels the

great glad ti - dings___ tell. O come, O come to us.___ A -

THE LIGHT OF CELEBRATION

NARRATOR I:

In the beginning was the Word, and the Word was with God, and the Word was God. He was with God in the beginning. Through Him all things were made. Without Him nothing was made that has been made. In Him was life, and that life was the light of all people. *(John 1:1-4)*

NARRATOR 2:

Let us therefore rejoice, for God, through Christ, has made us His children of Light. We are now a reflection of His glory. As we forsake the darkness of this world, we freely choose the illumination of God's truth and grace. Let us now shine our light before all people, so that by the light of our love, they may see the glory of God in all we say and do.

[Light the remaining candles.]

CAROLS OF CELEBRATION

Words by
JOSEPH M. MARTIN (BMI)

Based on tunes:
GLOUCESTERSHIRE WASSAIL
WASSAIL SONG
GOD REST YE MERRY GENTLEMEN
IN DULCI JUBILO, I SAW THREE SHIPS
and **ADESTE FIDELES**

Arranged by
JOSEPH M. MARTIN (BMI)

joice, let al - le - lu - ias ring. A -

wake, a - wake for the morn-ing is nigh. Dawn breaks with sing - ing and

ev-er-last-ing light, with ev-er-last-ing light. God sent us His Son. Re -

TAPESTRY OF '

joice, re-joice, for Je-sus has come.

Come and hear the glad-some song that fills the earth with

TAPESTRY OF LIGHT - SAT

grace.   Gath - er   at   the   man - ger   and   bring   a   gift   of

praise!   Sing   for   joy!   Praise   the   Lord!   Let   your

mu - sic   be   re - stored!   Sing   for   joy!____ Tell   the

* Tune: GOD REST YE MERRY GENTLEMEN, Traditional English Melody
Words: Traditional English

to the Lord sing prais - es, all you with - in this

mp unis.

and with true love and broth - er - hood, each

place;

oth - er now em - brace; for

mf

96

Christ is born in Beth - le - hem and comes to bring us grace. O___ ti - dings of com - fort and of joy, com-fort and joy. O___ ti - dings of com - fort and of

Tune: IN DULCI JUBILO, Traditional German Melody
Words: Traditional Latin, Tr. John Mason Neale, 1818-1866

TAPESTRY OF LIGHT - 9

TAPESTRY OF LIGHT - SAT

Tune: ADESTE FIDELES, John Francis Wade, 1710-1786
Words: Latin Hymn, John Francis Wade, 1710-1786, Tr. Frederick Oakeley, 1802-1880   TAPESTRY OF LIGHT -